LIAISONS
RE-IMAGINING SONDHEIM
FROM THE PIANO

Companion materials are necessary for three titles in this collection, and may be obtained online through the access code below. These include a second piano part for "Birds of Victorian England" and "Finishing the Hat – 2 Pianos," and an audio track for "Johanna in Space."

To access companion material online, visit:
www.halleonard.com/mylibrary
Enter Code
7177-1521-4214-6066

All pieces were commissioned expressly for The Liaisons Project, Rachel Colbert and Anthony de Mare, producers. Recorded by pianist Anthony de Mare on the ECM New Series CD set, *Liaisons: Re-Imagining Sondheim from the Piano*, ECM 2470-72.

ISBN 978-1-4950-7793-7

RILTING MUSIC, INC.

EXCLUSIVELY DISTRIBUTED BY
 HAL•LEONARD®
7777 W. BLUEMOUND RD. P.O. BOX 13819 MILWAUKEE, WI 53213

Visit Hal Leonard Online at
www.halleonard.com

CONTENTS ALPHABETICALLY BY TITLE

* Download second piano part online; see title page.

** Download companion audio track online; see title page.

CONTENTS ALPHABETICALLY BY COMPOSER

* Download second piano part online; see title page.

* Download second piano part online; see title page.
** Download companion audio track online; see title page.

ABOUT THE LIAISONS PROJECT

Adapted with permission from the liner notes to *Liaisons: Re-Imagining Sondheim from the Piano*, ECM 2470-72

Like many of us, I have long held in highest esteem the incomparable work of Stephen Sondheim, whose fearless eclecticism has emboldened many a musical risk-taker. Over the years I often found myself imagining how the many beloved songs of the Sondheim canon might sound if transformed into piano works. It then became apparent how much this resonated with the composers I'd worked with over the years. So at long last, in 2007, I began to pursue a formal commissioning project. With a generous spark of enthusiasm from Mr. S. and the partnership of a dedicated producer, **LIAISONS: Re-Imagining Sondheim from the Piano** was born.

Each composer has taken a distinct approach to the challenge of re-imagining. Some tell stories, some embark on journeys, some offer evocations of character and mood—yet always when I play them I hear the original song underneath. And if I were to be so bold as to offer one piece of advice to you, the pianist, it would be: to listen first to the original cast recording of the song being re-imagined. Subsequent versions may inform too, but begin with the original. It is the font from which this entire collection flows. However subtly, it will inform your fingers.

Presented in its entirety, this collection stands as a celebration of Sondheim as well as the composers who rose to the challenge of adding their voices to his, a creative alchemy that affirms that his work is as much at home in a concert hall as on a Broadway stage.

I have long imagined sharing this work with you. It's been said that all joy is the joy of discovery. I am excited and humbled to share some of the immense joy of discovery that the music presented here has brought me.

Sincerely,
—Anthony de Mare

Over the years I've heard songs of mine 'interpreted' by singers and piano-players and arrangers who change either the vocal lines or the harmonies, or both, and much as my ego gets a lift when people sing my stuff, in every case I've winced. The pieces created for *Liaisons* are a different matter entirely; they're written by composer, not arrangers, and they aren't decorations of the songs, they're fantasias on them, responses to the melodic lines and the harmonies and occasionally the accompaniments.

Some of the composers are friends, some I was familiar with musically but had never met, some were writers whose work was new to me. All of the pieces in the collection surprise me; they take approaches that would never have occurred to me. As you might expect, each approach is startlingly different from the others. It's fun (for me, anyway) to hear which of the song elements each composer latches on to, and how far they spin from them.

I'd like to take this opportunity to thank each of the composers for the care they put into their works. Their meticulousness is a pleasure (and a flattering one). And of course I have to thank Tony, not just for having the notion of 'Liaisons' in the first place, but for his perseverance in seeing it through to its conclusion (with unflagging support from Rachel Colbert, the producer of the project). It's not every pianist who has such imagination along with the passion, commitment and virtuoso technique, to carry it off.

—Stephen Sondheim

COMPOSER COMMENTS

Andy Akiho: The first time I listened to it, I loved the concept of *Into the Woods*—being lost in and confused by the woods, and the consistent and driving rhythms of the opening prologue. I was also intrigued by Sondheim's innovative and witty use of spoken narrative against his catchy melodies, particularly during each character's introduction. My goal in re-imagining this prologue was to orchestrate each character's personality with the use of prepared piano—for example, dimes on the strings for the cow scenes, poster tack on the strings for door knocks and narrated phrases, and credit card string-clusters for the wicked witch. My goal was to portray each character's story and mystical journey using exotic piano timbres in place of text.

Mason Bates: The manic energy of Sondheim's "Putting It Together"—which showcases the collision of art and schmoozing at a spectacular art opening—seemed an intriguing challenge to compress into a piano solo. The two primary themes of the scene are, well, put together here— smashed together, actually—in a quicksilver showpiece for one of the most gifted and inventive pianists, Anthony de Mare.

Eve Beglarian: "Perpetual Happiness" is a reworking of the opening duet from *Passion*, sung by two lovers who will not end up staying together. I am fascinated at how Sondheim has written a perfectly realized romantic duet while simultaneously undercutting the permanence of that love, embodying both the devotion and the falsity in the relationship. I used nothing but the notes of the original piano/vocal, arrayed as a virtuoso *moto perpetuo* for Tony as a way of exploring and illuminating how the musical materials of the original create their subtle commentary on the illusions of superficial romantic love.

Derek Bermel: "Sorry/Grateful" has always been one of my favorite Sondheim songs; it embodies so deeply the vagaries of the human heart. At times I found it physically painful to rip the music away from its perfectly harmonious lyrics. But I tried valiantly to preserve the ruminative and yearning quality of the original for Tony. My "Sorry/Grateful" is exactly 80 bars long, in tribute to Steve. Here's to the next 40 measures!

Jherek Bischoff: My very good friend and frequent collaborator Jen Goma turned me on to "Ballad of Guiteau." When I mentioned this project to her (the biggest Sondheim fan ever!), she said I should check it out. I was not familiar with this particular piece before and I am so happy to have found it! I immediately knew that I could have a lot of fun with this piece. It's kind of like two separate pieces running parallel to each other and switching back and forth, with moments of emptiness, and moments of bombastic energy. This is my first arrangement for solo piano, and what a treat that it is in Mr. de Mare's hands!

William Bolcom: The main theme for "A Little Night Fughetta" is taken from "Anyone Can Whistle," a melody that struck me as a fugue subject—with a countersubject of "Send in the Clowns." I thought Steve would be amused at a fugue-like, and mercifully short, piece. Thus a fughetta and not a fugue.

Jason Robert Brown: "Green Finch and Linnet Bird" has had a mesmeric hold on me since I first heard it when I was ten years old. While the whole of *Sweeney Todd* is transfixing, these particular two and a half minutes seem to me distinct from the rest of Sondheim's entire canon— the structure, turning in on itself with every repetition; the harmonic language, pushing away from the tonic in spite of its singsongy melody; the baroquely poetic but naïve lyric—a musical masterpiece. Towards the end of the song, there is a trill notated for the singer (a trill which I have never heard executed well), and that seemed like a good starting point for the journey of this particular arrangement. I pictured Johanna in a room filled with trilling birds, and decided to paint portraits of the birds rather than their mistress. Fairly early on, I realized that what I was hoping to do wouldn't be possible with only two hands, so there are four piano parts (three recorded). For this publication I adapted it, for practical reasons, for two pianos.

Kenji Bunch: My first exposure to *Sweeney Todd* came as a 10-year old watching a PBS broadcast of the Broadway production. I was both terrified and fascinated, and have felt the work's and Sondheim's influence ever since. For "The Demon Barber"—an homage to the seething, menacing introductory song, "The Ballad of Sweeney Todd," I highlighted the original song's oblique references to the "Dies Irae" Gregorian melody into a persistent, ominous chant that surfaces throughout. I also wanted to amplify the work's horror-show qualities with low register rumblings, shrieking high clusters, and insistent rhythmic ostinato patterns.

Mary Ellen Childs: In the lyrics of "Now-Later-Soon," I love the way Sondheim, in the end, turns "Now" into "Later," "Later" to "Soon" and "Soon" to "Now," turning everything on its head. My version is mostly "Now," with a little bit of "Later" and "Soon" sprinkled here and there, my way of mixing "Now" and "Later" and "Soon" together. These words refer to time, so I decided to play with the meter. Since this piece and all of *A Little Night Music* is in various meters of three, it seemed especially inviting to tweak the meter with sevens and fives, truncating here extending there, momentarily lurching forward or drawing out, all while simultaneously flowing along.

Michael Daugherty: When I got the call to compose my opera *Jackie O* (1993) for the Houston Grand Opera, I began my research by listening to Sammy Davis Jr. recordings and attending a performance of Stephen Sondheim's masterpiece *Assassins*. For decades, I have been a great admirer of Mr. Sondheim's uncanny ability to fuse witty, brilliant, complex lyrics with original, beautiful, catchy music. *Assassins* is a personal favorite of mine and "Everybody's Got the Right" finds Mr. Sondheim at his very best. I take the signature Sondheim chords from the beginning of "Everybody's Got the Right" and spin my own cluster chords, which finally explode like a volley of gunfire. I also incorporate fragments from "Hail to the Chief" to remind us of the numerous assassinations from Lincoln to Kennedy.

Peter Golub: I chose "Children and Art" because I believe it is a beautiful and profound song, one that "says it all." Having made the choice my real troubles began. How do you take something that is complete and perfectly realized and then think you have something to add to it. Just playing the piano/vocal score is really all you need. That's a pretty tenacious monkey to have on one's back. But I eventually realized I had to make my own thing out of it and not feel encumbered by the perfection of the original. I make ample use of the main melody and I follow the harmonic structure of the original but I've written a piece in my own voice, one that expands on the song in a pianistic way.

Ricky Ian Gordon: In 1973, when Stephen Sondheim's *A Little Night Music* was running on Broadway, I was 17 years old. I was obsessed with it. . . I saw it six times. There was one song though, every time I saw it, which I never tired of, that I couldn't wait to hear at every show—"Every Day A Little Death"—this perfect blend of words and music, this beautiful poem of a song, this energetic elegy on the humiliations of love. As far as what I did for Tony, well, I didn't even look at the music—I just started riffing on what I myself might like to play, as if I were playing that song for someone, introducing its delicate intricacies, its stunning melody and the counter melody of the duet. For when one plays from the original vocal score, all one is playing is the accompaniment . . . while here, I tried, from my memory of it, to have the fingers play everything. I took some things out of their original time, and meter . . . I guess you could say, I sort of made love to it, with gratitude for all the pleasure it had given me, as well as the rest of Mr. Sondheim's monumental body of work.

Annie Gosfield: I was honored to be invited to re-imagine one of Stephen Sondheim's works for Anthony de Mare. I chose "A Bowler Hat" because of its unusual theme both musically and in terms of narrative. It is from *Pacific Overtures*, and features a repeated theme that is beautifully constructed, very catchy, and a little melancholy. The subject of the musical is the difficult Westernization of Japan, told from the point of view of the Japanese. I was intrigued by this unusual song, and as a former milliner, the reference to the bowler hat made it a perfect match for me.

Jake Heggie: "I'm Excited. No, You're Not." is my take on Stephen Sondheim's amazing ensemble, "A Weekend in the Country." I tried to capture the energy and the momentum, as well as a few bumps in the road, in creating a big, fun, splashy tour-de-force for Tony de Mare.

Fred Hersch: "No One Is Alone" (from *Into the Woods*) appealed to me because its diatonic melody (like many of the great tunes by Richard Rodgers) enabled me to make subtle changes in the harmony that reflect my jazz sensibility. I could make the arrangement sound lush and pianistic—and just let the melody sing. And I love what the lyric says—it is a very relevant song.

Ethan Iverson: Some songs we never tire of no matter how many times we hear them. My reasonably straightforward arrangement of "Send in the Clowns" can be played on a concert grand but might be even better on a barroom upright. The original melody at the beginning recurs and interferes, eventually provoking a humiliating outburst in G major (instead of the correct G minor).

Gabriel Kahane: "Being Alive" begins as a scherzo of sorts, taking Sondheim's "doorbell" motif and contorting it into various humorous guises before the appearance of the tune in a fractured chorale, followed by a series of reharmonizations. The doorbell motif reappears as a transition to the bridge of the original song, which I've reimagined here as an homage to Ligeti's first piano étude, "Désordre." Finally, the main tune returns triumphantly in bitonal guise, giving way to an emotionally ambiguous coda.

Phil Kline: Shortly after confirming that my piece would be based on "Someone in a Tree" the worries began. What had I gotten myself into? Can I really have chosen a song that answers the eternal question: what really happened at the signing of the US-Japan treaty of 1854? A song that's not even a song per se but an ensemble, a quartet no less, two of whose members are the same person at different times? A song not about romance but history itself, perception, memory, the futility of narrative and . . . I forgot what I was saying . . . Oh yes, there's the part about it being a miracle. "Someone in a Tree" is far too big and teeming and elusive to be captured in a single gesture, or even a few. It derives so much excitement from the discovery of its process that the only way to go is to rediscover it, follow the trajectory from point to point, more or less, and make humble observations about the details along the way. The pebble not the stream, you know.

Tania León: "going … gone" is a mosaic of exuberant rapid passages of gradual intensity, harmonic plateaus, rhythmical motions and subtle chords imitations derived from musical references of Sondheim's "Good Thing Going." The periodic interruptions by echoes of unexpected interactions of 19th century classic Cuban dances act as a bridge between different sections of the work.

Ricardo Lorenz: Summer of 1982 was wonderfully diabolic. As a newly arrived foreign student from Venezuela assigned to the Indiana University Opera chorus, I danced a waltz with Mephistopheles and had my throat slit by the demon barber of Fleet Street. The truth is that singing in Gounod's *Faust* that summer dressed like a monk was great, but it didn't compare to the experience of singing in *Sweeney Todd*—my first encounter with the powerful world of Stephen Sondheim. In honor of this masterpiece, "The Worst [Empanadas] in London" is a re-imagining of "The Worst Pies in London" and "A Little Priest" as a tongue-in-cheek, smorgasbord of Latin American grooves, preserving as much as possible the original features and intent of these songs. I am deeply indebted to the late Fredda Hyman and to Music in the Loft for commissioning this work especially for The Liaisons Project.

Wynton Marsalis: Stephen Sondheim employs many syncopated and expressive devices in "That Old Piano Roll." My arrangement uses these concepts to evoke the styles of three great jazz pianists. The basic stride style of James P. Johnson is answered by the jagged, obtuse style of Thelonious Monk. Both find resolution in the ragtime-swing style of New Orleans pianist Jelly Roll Morton. The parlor piano elegance of the second theme, with its tresillo rhythm, is juxtaposed to a 4/4 New Orleans ragtime stomp. In the 1920s a heated debate swirled around jazz as polite society music or red hot dance music. Now, we happily play it all.

Paul Moravec: "I Think About You" takes its title from the second—and oft-repeated line of "Losing My Mind" from Follies. In my reimagining for piano solo, the eponymous musical phrase repeats maniacally to the point of "losing its mind." The piece is a musical meditation on obsession, heartbreak, and, finally, the timeless need to love and be loved.

Nico Muhly: The light-suffused chords that open *Sunday in the Park with George* are some of the best-spaced chords ever. I used to obsessively study them and play them and dream about ways to steal them. What is particularly astonishing about *Sunday*, too, is the way in which the "mechanical" music that drives the score gives way to an emotional immediacy with the characters instantly: it's the best tension between the motor and the heart. This is clearest, I think, in "Color and Light," a multi-part duet between George and Dot and, indeed, the orchestra. My homage to this piece tries to accentuate the angular music, making it somewhat dangerously unhinged, while always returning to the more supple landscape of the love story.

John Musto: "Epiphany" begins with a fidgety solo line of underscoring, which appears just after Sweeney Todd's first murder (of Pirelli the barber), his first realization that he can dispatch someone coolly and efficiently. Many of the quotations reference the loss of his wife, Lucy. The taunting music of the insane Lucy serves as a descant to Todd's doleful narrative—"There was a barber and his wife . . ." The beggar woman's pathetic lament—"Alms, alms, for a pitiful woman . . ." courses throughout. "Epiphany" is a feverish dreamscape—shards of Sweeney's memories and nightmares, thrown together in a crucible of counterpoint.

Thomas Newman: *Sweeney Todd* always lifts me into the dusty attic of my youth and a time of profound musical questioning. And if I asked . . . Steve's answers to me were never obvious, always thoughtful and uniquely observed. Beyond his enduring talents and imagination, he was always the most natural and gifted teacher. Brilliantly refined, verbally expressive. But what focus! And how generous! This version of "Not While I'm Around" is another dialogue, I suppose, another attempt at creative engagement. This time, though, in simple, poignant harmony and shared phrase.

David Rakowski: Like all of the composers in The Liaisons Project, I was presented with the problem of reframing a song that is already perfect—and in my case, my favorite Sondheim song, "The Ladies Who Lunch." My solution was, to the best of my ability, to concentrate on the character's deep sadness, thereby eschewing the song's big finish for a slow, introspective one.

Steve Reich: "Finishing the Hat — 2 Pianos" for Stephen Sondheim is a rather faithful re-working of one of Sondheim's favorite songs from *Sunday in the Park with George*, and incidentally the title of his recent book. Harmonically very close to the original, and melodically adding only occasional variations, my only real change is in the rhythm of constantly changing meters. This gives my two piano version a rhythmic character more in line with my own music and, hopefully, another perspective with which to appreciate Sondheim's brilliant original.

Eric Rockwell: I tried to keep the craziness to a minimum in "You Could Drive a Person Crazy," opting instead to create a straight-ahead piano arrangement of Sondheim's wonderful song. I picture it taking place in a cabaret room where the patrons are loud and drunk and not really listening to the pianist. As a result, he occasionally tries to catch someone's ear by channeling his inner Liberace as well as other assorted demons lurking inside him. The result is what I call a "Schizo Scherzo."

Daniel Bernard Roumain: When the brilliant pianist Anthony de Mare asked me to participate in his Liaisons Project, I was scared. I was asked to take something sacred (a song by Stephen Sondheim) and arrange it for piano. I tried for several weeks to make "Another Hundred People" work, and nothing worked. Finally, after a late-night conversation with Anthony, he encouraged me to simply "duet" with the music, and have a conversation with Mr. Sondheim's score. That's what I did.

Frederic Rzewski: My friend—almost a brother—Steve ben Israel, whom I knew for almost 50 years, died recently. The thought "I'm Still Here" hit me in a way I had never known. That's when I wrote this arrangement of Stephen Sondheim's great song. I stuck rigorously to the song's structure. It helped me to get feelings out which I would not have been able to express otherwise.

Rodney Sharman: "Notes on 'Beautiful,'" commissioned by Anthony de Mare through the generosity of the Banff Centre for the Arts, was written in the Valentine Studio, Leighton Arts Colony, Banff, Alberta. The piece is a transformation of the duet "Beautiful" between mother and son, from *Sunday in the Park with George*, and dedicated to Anthony de Mare and the memory of my mother."

Duncan Sheik: By some happy twist of circumstance my mother took me to see the original Broadway production on *Sweeney Todd* when I was 9 years old. I remember a shocking amount of blood. Returning to see the show in John Doyle's 2006 production I more fully appreciated the neat trick of how Johanna morphs from a plaintive, hopeful declaration of love into the pathos and pathology of love completely lost. Two opposite ends of the human condition oscillating back and forth. Not being a virtuoso pianist myself I wanted to simplify the actual piano part to its most basic components—the Satie version of "Johanna" if you will. But I also wanted to have the atmosphere of Johanna's celestial beauty and the idea that, like a shooting star, she is out of reach. To this end I employed a technique of layering dozens of takes of guitar improvisation through a tape echo thus creating a blanket of sound for the piano to linger within. So a piece for piano and tape echo, "Johanna in Space."

David Shire: My arrangement of "Love Is in the Air" takes the piece through some ragtime and jazz territory. The quote from "Comedy Tonight" is a reference, of course, to the number which replaced "Love Is in the Air" as the opening to *A Funny Thing Happened on the Way to the Forum*. The first time I heard "Love Is in the Air" was when Steve played it for me, soon after we first met, while he was writing *Forum*. What an indelible and treasured memory that is.

Bernadette Speach: Throughout "In and Out of Love," the essential harmonies from "Liaisons" and "Send in the Clowns" are juxtaposed and transformed, and interact as pillars upon which the phrases and melodies from both songs are recalled and remembered. The meter is in three, reflecting the original songs. It is my hope that this new work will convey the feelings and memories of the magical dance of love within the original songs, as well as to express the profound impact of their revelations on my life.

Mark-Anthony Turnage: I have loved *Sweeney Todd* from the first time I heard it. It's almost perfect and so full of beautiful stage craft and amazing invention. It's hard to pick a highlight but I was thrilled that "Pretty Women" was still available to mess around with. It's memorable, sophisticated and above all strangely moving. Very humbling for me to get a chance to write "Stephen Sondheim arranged Mark-Anthony Turnage" at the top of the score.

Nils Vigeland: My transcription is of two songs from the 1981 show, *Merrily We Roll Along*— the title song and the opening number "The Hills of Tomorrow." Sequentially, the music follows that of the show itself except I bring the alma mater ("Behold the hills . . .") back at the end, just as it occurs at the very end of the actual show. The great challenge and joy of working with Sondheim's music, is that it does not in my view admit of harmonic alteration, it's already perfect, so that finding "new notes" to make it piano music required the discovery of a contrapuntal principle of elaboration. A single three-note voice leading serves as the vehicle for finding these new notes.

COMMISSIONING CREDITS

**All pieces were commissioned expressly for The Liaisons Project,
Rachel Colbert and Anthony de Mare, Producers**

COMPOSER	TITLE	COMMISSIONED BY
Andy Akiho	Into the Woods	Bob and Anna Livingston
Mason Bates	Very Put Together	James and Ellen Marcus and Annaliese Soros, for the wedding of Beth Sapery and Rosita Sarnoff
Eve Beglarian	Perpetual Happiness	Jeannie Colbert, for Rachel Colbert and Murphy Guyer
Derek Bermel	Sorry/Grateful	Tom Spain, for Anthony/Tony
William Bolcom	A Little Night Fughetta	William E. Terry
Jason Robert Brown	Birds of Victorian England	Anthony Razzano and the de Mare family
Kenji Bunch	The Demon Barber	The Clarice Smith Performing Arts Center
Mary Ellen Childs	Now	The Schubert Club
Michael Daugherty	Everybody's Got the Right	The Gilmore International Keyboard Festival
Peter Golub	A Child of Children and Art	Beth Rudin DeWoody, for Kyle DeWoody
Ricky Ian Gordon	Every Day a Little Death	Ted and Mary Jo Shen
Jake Heggie	I'm Excited. No You're Not.	The Clarice Smith Performing Arts Center
Fred Hersch	No One Is Alone	Dan Gallagher and Peter Shearer, for their son Ian Gallagher Shearer
Ethan Iverson	Send in the Clowns	Frank K. Godchaux and Mark Murashige
Gabriel Kahane	Being Alive	Ted and Mary Jo Shen
Phil Kline	Paraphrase (Someone in a Tree)	William E. Terry
Tania León	going….gone	Scott and Roxanne Bok
Ricardo Lorenz	The Worst [Empanadas] in London	Music in the Loft, Chicago
Wynton Marsalis	That Old Piano Roll	Bob and Anna Livingston
Paul Moravec	I Think About You	Martin L. and Lucy Miller Murray
Nico Muhly	Color and Light	Ted and Mary Jo Shen
John Musto	Epiphany	Martin and Perry Granoff
Thomas Newman	Not While I'm Around	James and Ellen Marcus
David Rakowski	The Ladies Who Lunch	Beth Rudin DeWoody
Steve Reich	Finishing the Hat – 2 Pianos	Ben and Donna Rosen
Eric Rockwell	You Could Drive a Person Crazy	Beth Rudin DeWoody, for Carlton DeWoody
Daniel Bernard Roumain	Another Hundred People	Heather and Justin Frank, M.D.
Frederic Rzewski	I'm Still Here	The Clarice Smith Performing Arts Center
Rodney Sharman	Notes on "Beautiful"	The Banff Centre
Duncan Sheik	Johanna in Space	Richard and Linda Sweetnam, in memory of Anthony Razzano
David Shire	Love Is in the Air	Ben and Donna Rosen
Bernadette Speach	In and Out of Love	The Clarice Smith Performing Arts Center
Mark-Anthony Turnage	Pretty Women	David and Alice Shearer
Nils Vigeland	Merrily We Roll Along	Beth Rudin DeWoody, for Darian Zahedi

The Ballad of Guiteau

after "The Ballad of Guiteau" from *Assassins*
By Stephen Sondheim and Jherek Bischoff

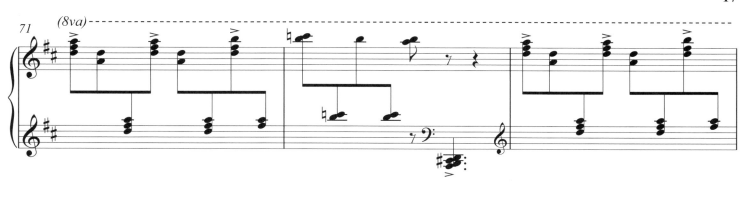

Sing this melody! NO PIANO!

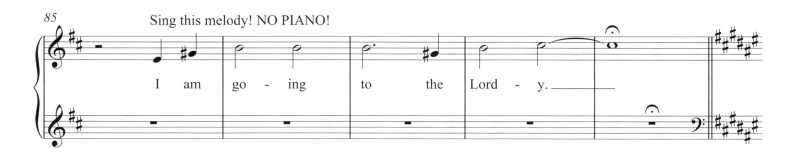

I am go - ing to the Lord - y. ___

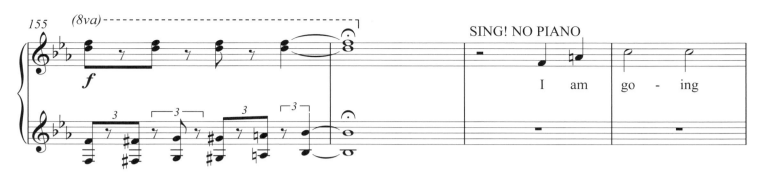

SING! NO PIANO

I am go - ing

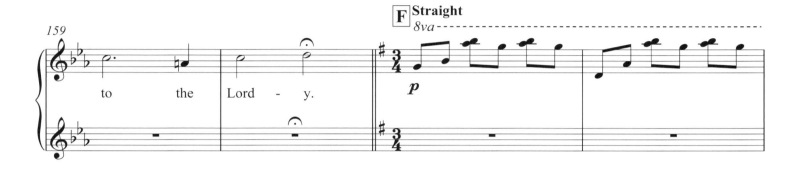

to the Lord - y.

F **Straight**

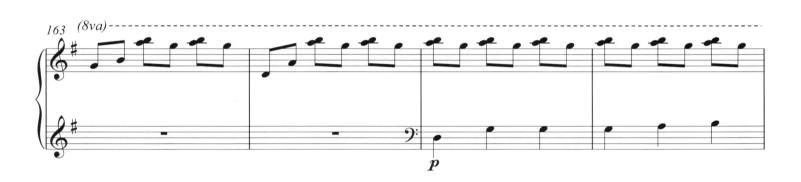

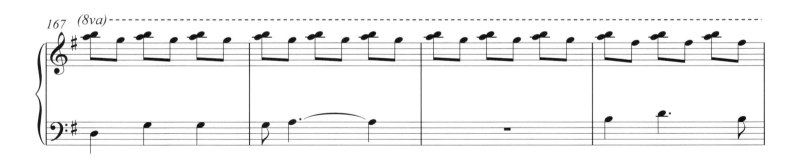

OMINOUSLY!

molto crescendo

slam the lid of the piano down, and make creaking sounds with the piano bench, if it allows those sounds... fella was just hung :(*

*OPTIONAL ENDING: Use a pre-recorded "swinging gallows" sound effect, played immediately following the slamming of the lid.

Another Hundred People

after "Another Hundred People" from *Company*
By Stephen Sondheim and Daniel Bernard Roumain
(Optional Improv-Cadenza by Anthony de Mare)

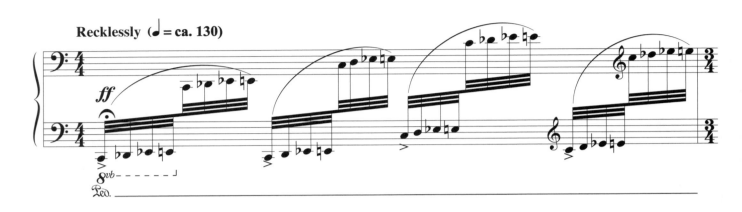

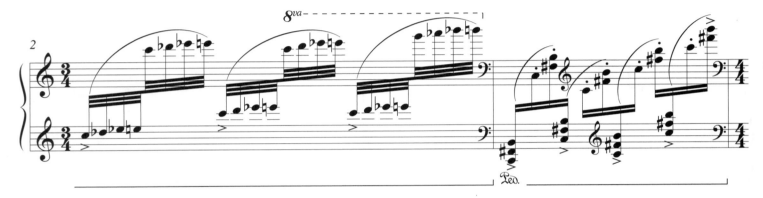

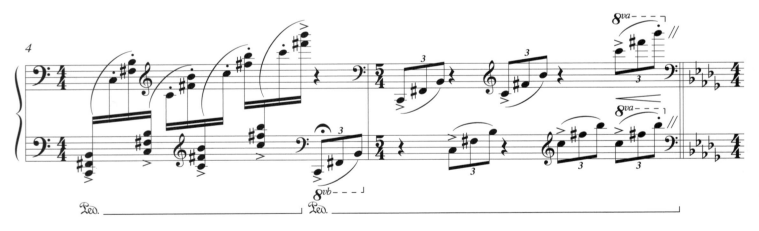

Optional 'Improv-Cadenza'

rallentando un poco

Poco meno mosso ($\quarternote = 138 / \halfnote = 69$)

Poco meno mosso (♩ = 60-63)

End of Optional 'Improv-Cadenza'

poco ritard.

A tempo (♩ = 132)

(free pedaling)

22 July 2011
Dover, MA

Revised
May 2016

For Ted and Mary Jo Shen

Being Alive

after "Being Alive" from *Company*
By Stephen Sondheim and Gabriel Kahane

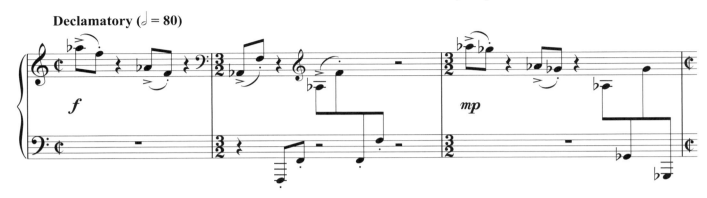

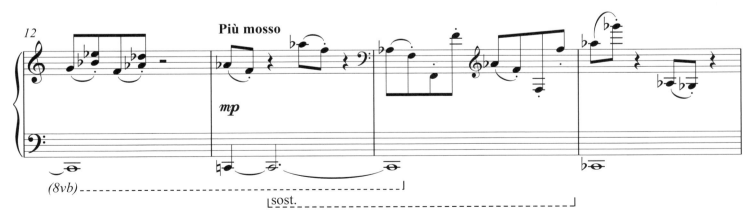

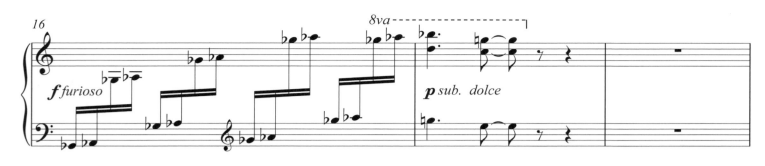

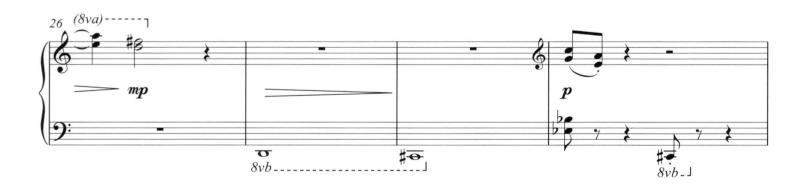

Brooklyn, NY April-May 2011

Birds of Victorian England

after "Green Finch and Linnet Bird" from *Sweeney Todd*
By Stephen Sondheim and Jason Robert Brown

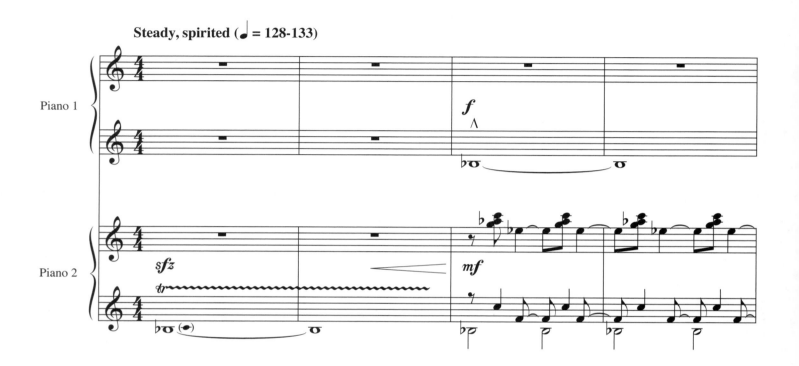

* See title page for an access code for www.halleonard.com/mylibrary to print a second piano part.

Crisply, mischievously

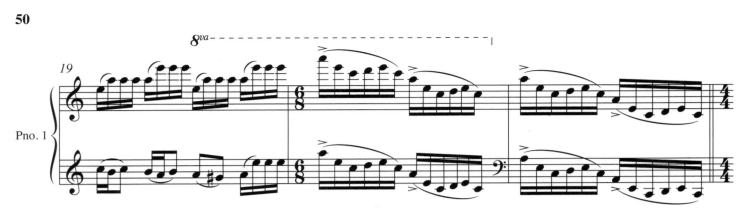

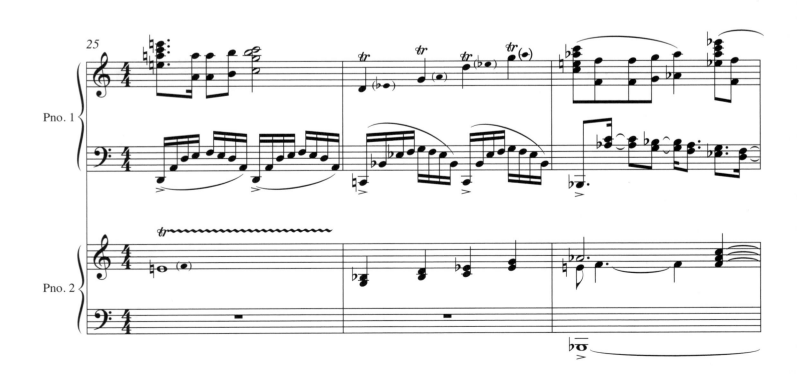

Aggressive, mechanical

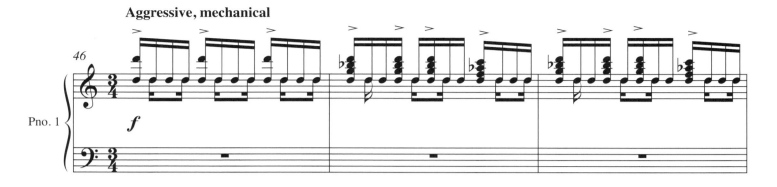

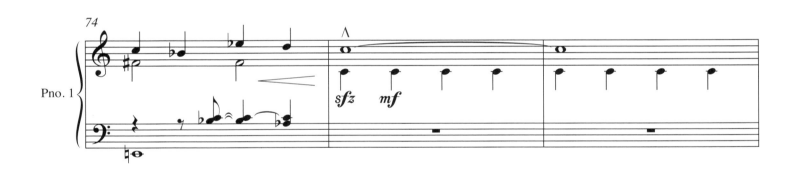

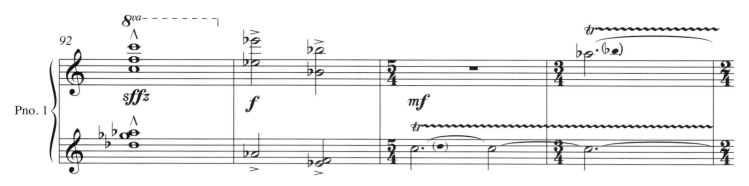

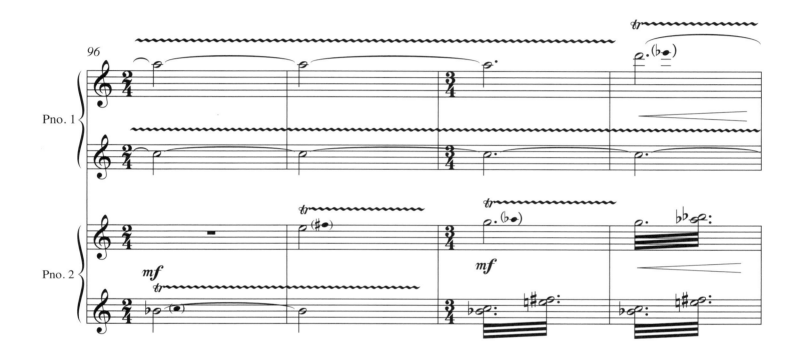

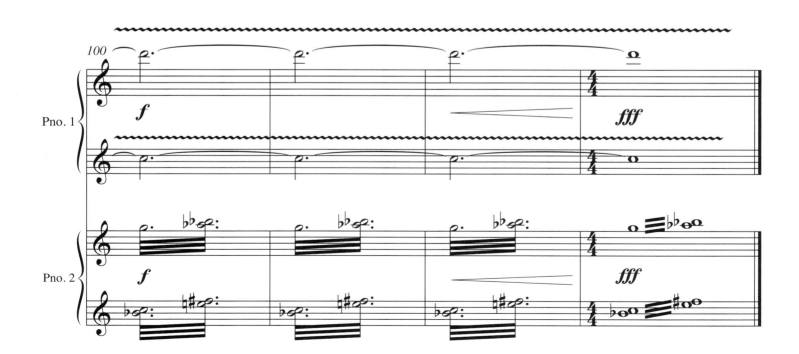

A Bowler Hat

after "A Bowler Hat" from *Pacific Overtures*
By Stephen Sondheim and Annie Gosfield

Dynamics below the staff only refer to the left hand.
Dynamics marked (RH) only refer to the right hand.
Only the first dynamic in a group will be marked (RH) (as in m. 32–34).
RH or LH (without parentheses) refers to which hand plays the selected notes.

Commissioned by Beth Rudin de Woody for Kyle de Woody
as part of The Liaisons Project of pianist Anthony de Mare.

A Child of Children and Art

after "Children and Art" from *Sunday in the Park with George*
By Stephen Sondheim and Peter Golub

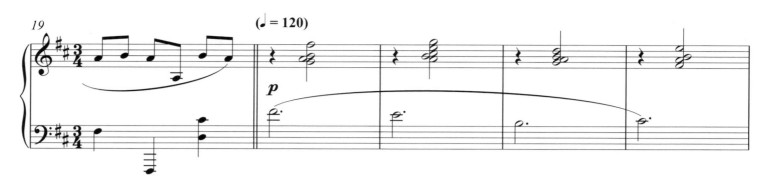

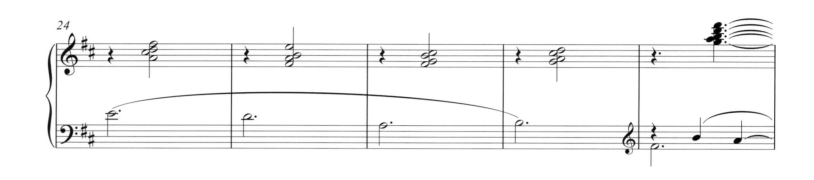

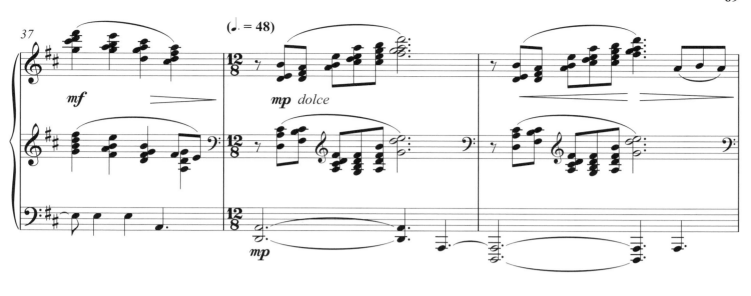

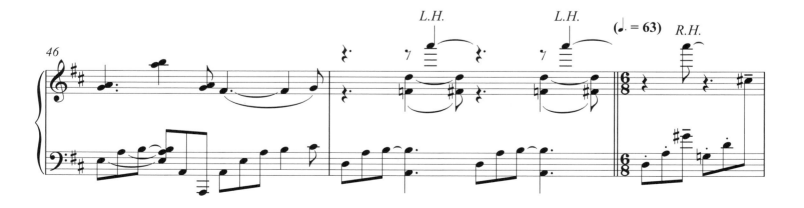

Color and Light

after "Color and Light" from *Sunday in the Park with George*
By Stephen Sondheim and Nico Muhly

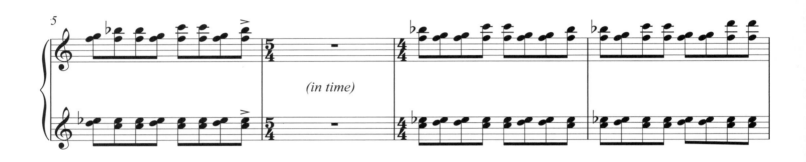

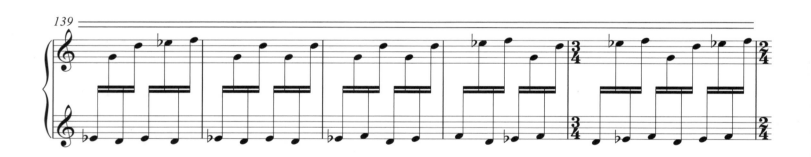

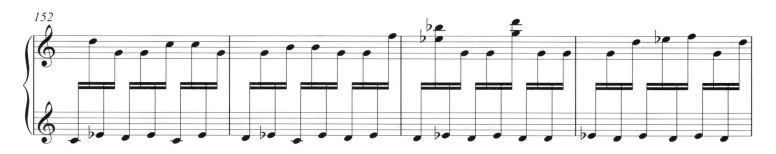

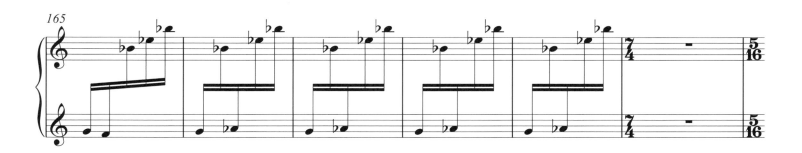

Slightly Relaxed (♩ = 120)

upper notes slightly to the fore

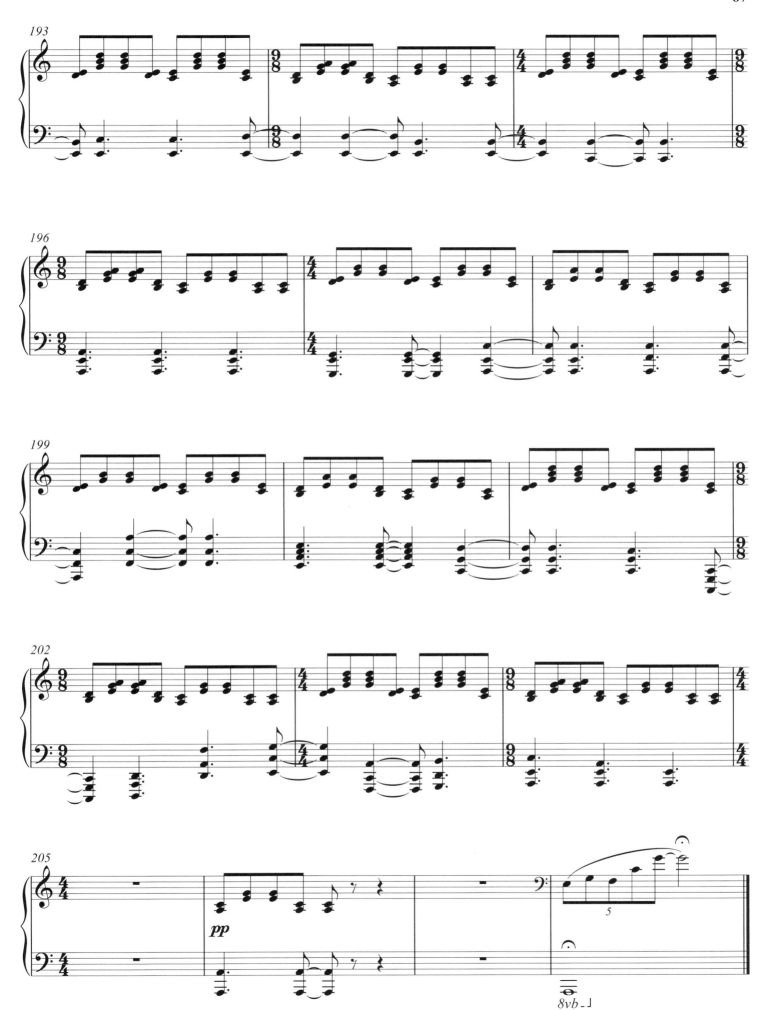

Commissioned for Anthony de Mare by Liaisons: Re-imagining Sondheim for the piano

The Demon Barber

after "The Ballad of Sweeney Todd" from *Sweeney Todd*
By Stephen Sondheim and Kenji Bunch

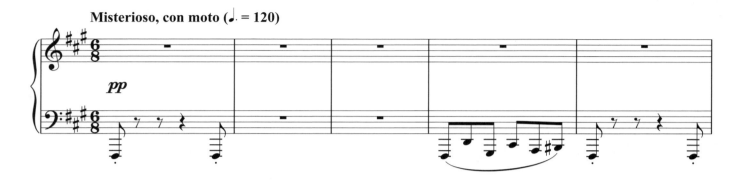

96

Everybody's Got the Right

after "Everybody's Got the Right" from *Assassins*
By Stephen Sondheim and Michael Daugherty

"Everybody's Got the Right"

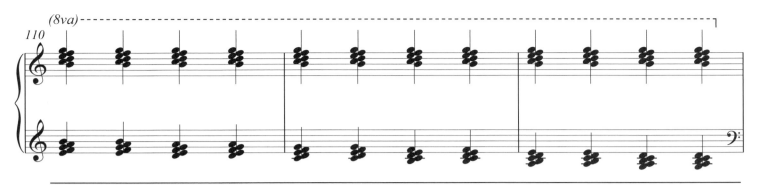

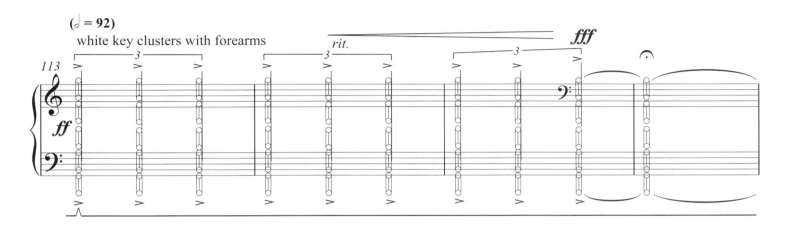

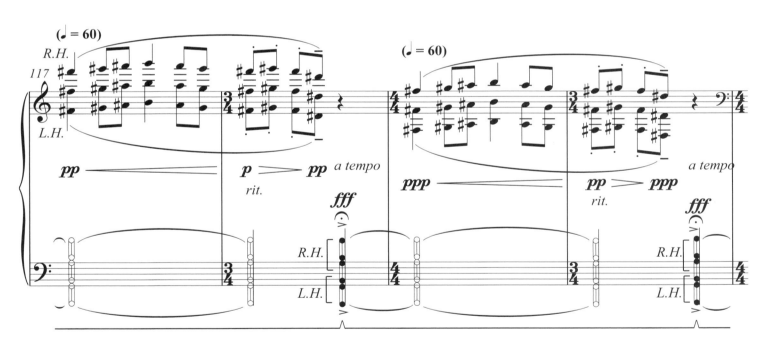

Optional:
Slowly take hidden
theater prop gun and
aim above audience

Fire gun with right hand
simultaneously with chord

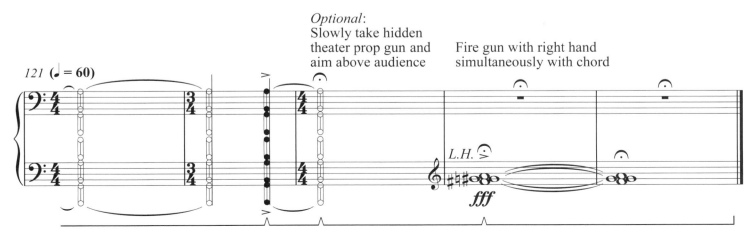

Epiphany

after music from *Sweeney Todd*
By Stephen Sondheim and John Musto

Sost. Ped.

Take silently in S. P.

Sost. Ped.

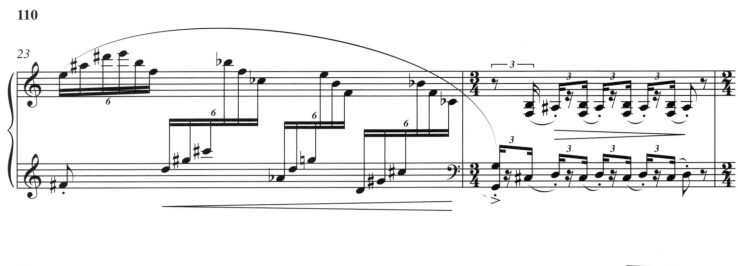

Every Day a Little Death

after "Every Day a Little Death" from *A Little Night Music*
By Stephen Sondheim and Ricky Ian Gordon

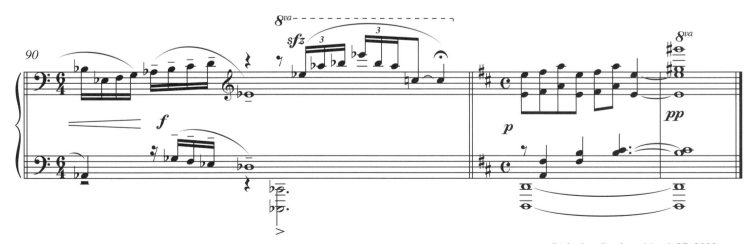

Ricky Ian Gordon, March 27, 2008
(revised Noveber 30, 2009 and then
September 1st, 2010)

for Stephen Sondheim

Finishing the Hat – 2 Pianos

after "Finishing the Hat" from *Sunday in the Park with George*
By Stephen Sondheim and Steve Reich

See title page for an access code for www.halleonard.com/mylibrary to print a second piano part.

Shavat 16, 5770
January 31, 2010

I Think About You

after "Losing My Mind" from *Follies*
By Stephen Sondheim and Paul Moravec

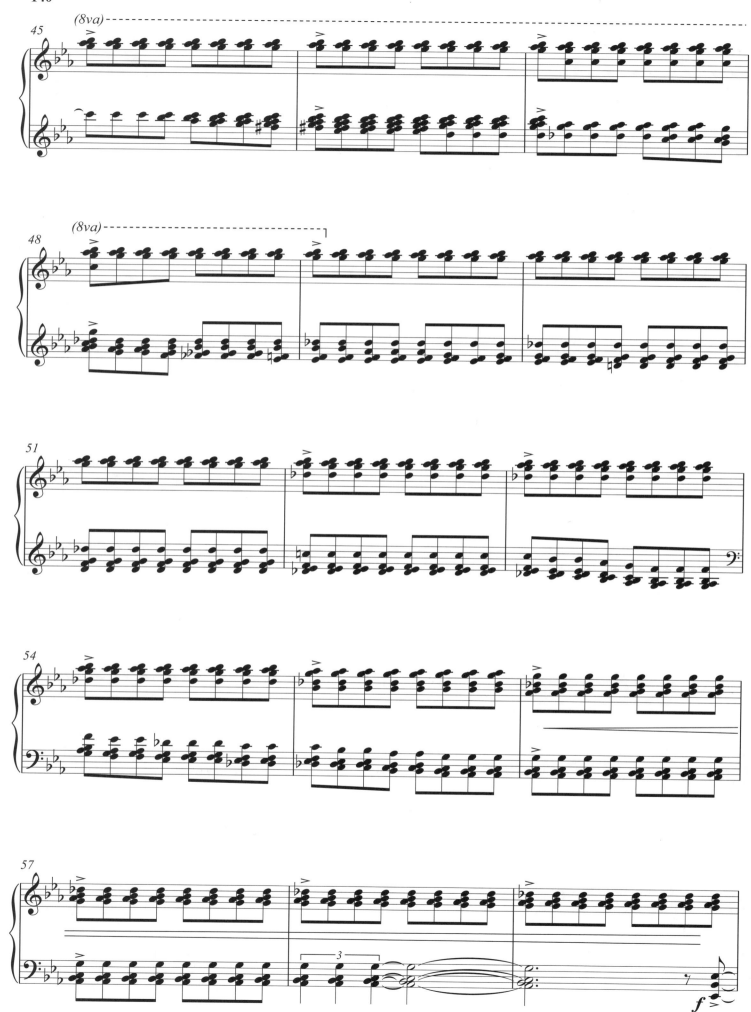

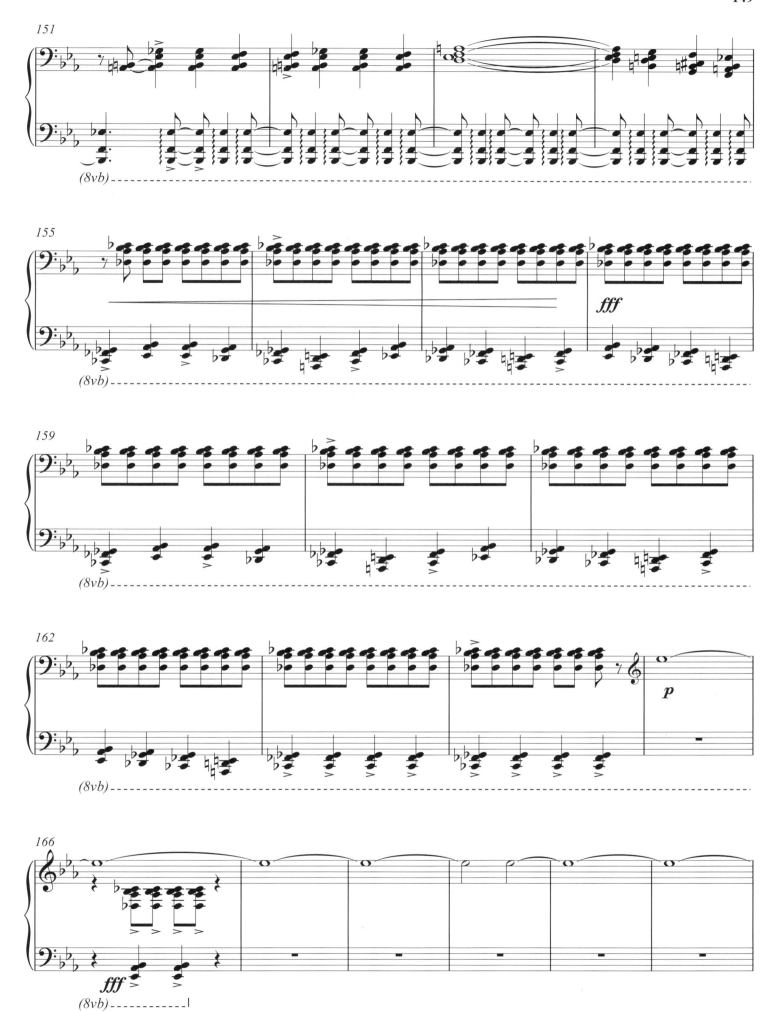

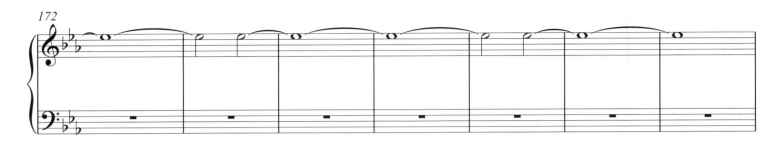

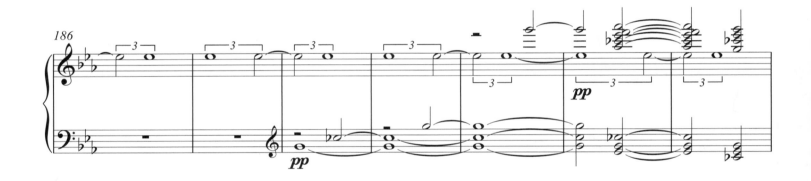

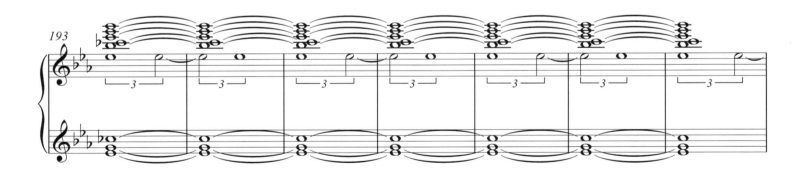

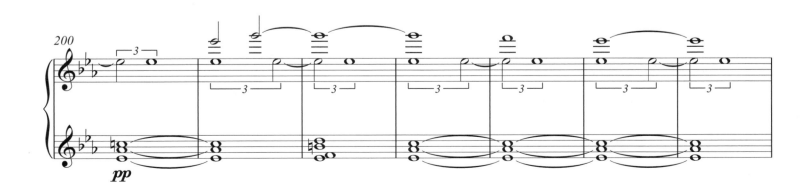

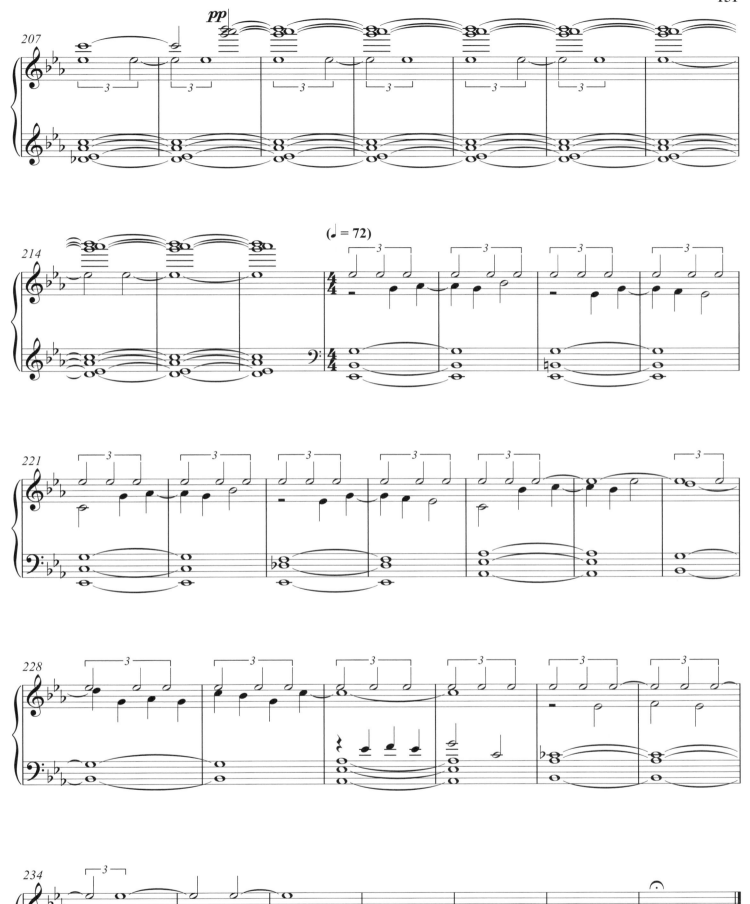

to Anthony de Mare and Stephen Sondheim

going... gone

after "Good Thing Going" from *Merrily We Roll Along*
By Stephen Sondheim and Tania León

Danzon espressivo (♩ = 68)

flowing forward

ritmico preciso (♩ = 88)

Danzon - Habanera
dolce, molto rubato

I'm Excited. No, You're Not.

after "A Weekend in the Country" from *A Little Night Music*
By Stephen Sondheim and Jake Heggie

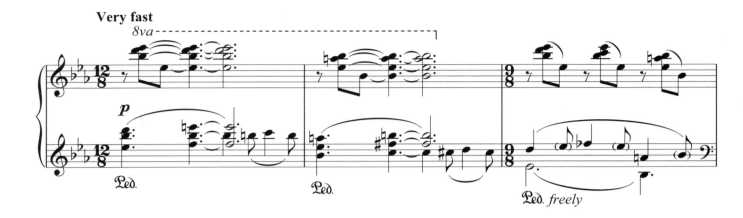

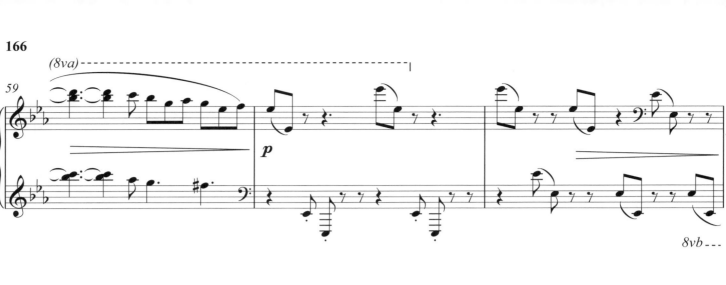

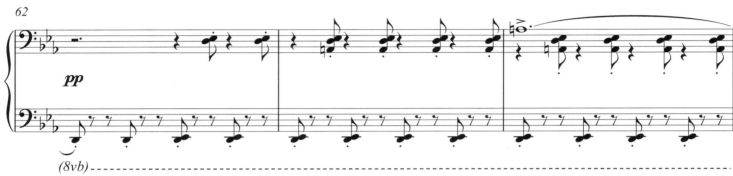

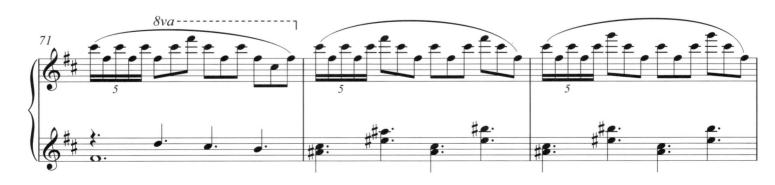

I'm Still Here

after "I'm Still Here" from *Follies*
By Stephen Sondheim and Frederic Rzewski

*End **ppp**, hold very briefly with pedal.

Into the Woods

— Piano Preparations —

Preparation Requirements:

Poster Tack: D^2, E^2, C^4, & B^7 – C^8 | 3 Dimes: E^4, G^4, B^5 | 2 Credit Cards

---

Poster Tack

Press firmly into strings

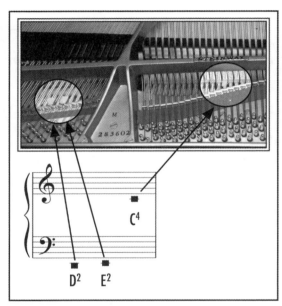

Dime Preparation:

Weave dime between strings on far bridge; away from hammers. Keep the dimes as close to the bridge as possible. Prepared notes should maintain fundamental pitches.

Extended Credit Card Techniques:

Long gliss. on strings
with Credit Card

Short gliss. up strings
with Credit Card

String Cluster
with Credit Card

Scrape Pins
with Credit Card

Into the Woods

after Act I Opening from *Into the Woods*
By Stephen Sondheim and Andy Akiho

Risoluto (♩ = 128-132)

Spoken with articulate conviction and clarity: *"Once Upon a Time!"*

(accent - loud pedal attack with foot)

(accent - loud pedal attack with foot)

(Sequence: Maj 7ths up chromatic starting on G) ⟶

(pedal sempre) →

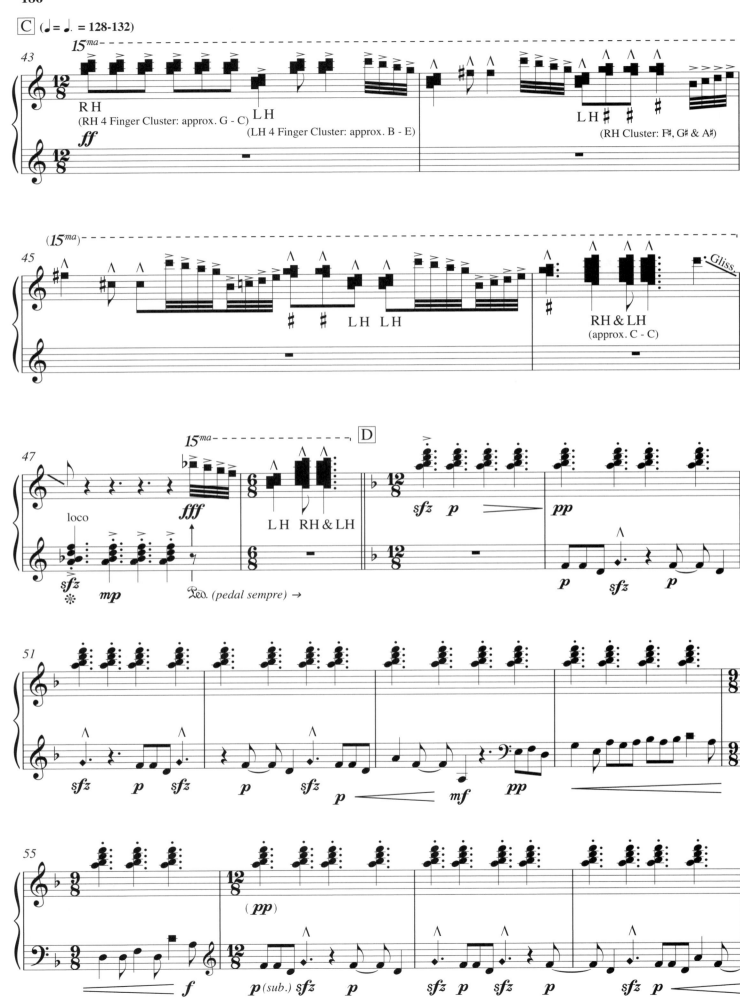

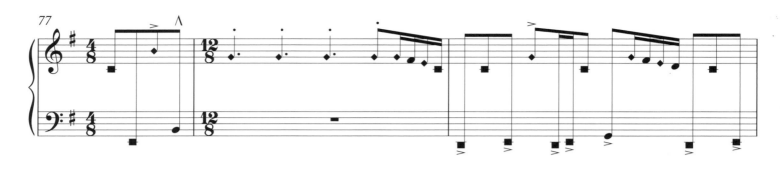

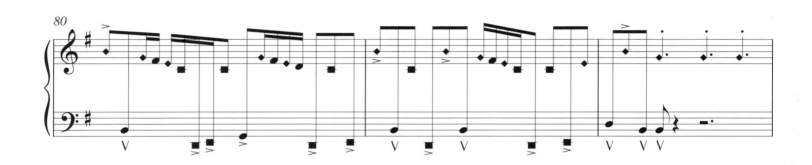

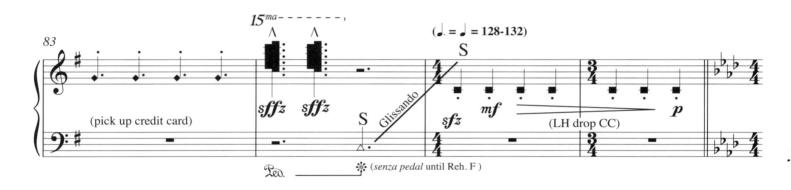

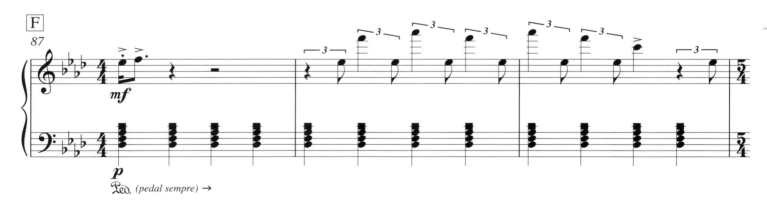

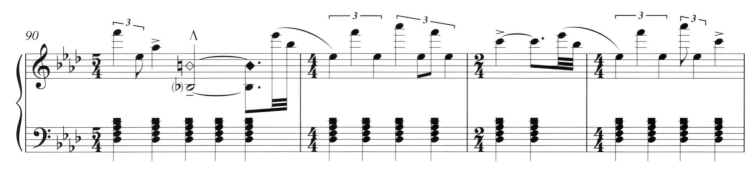

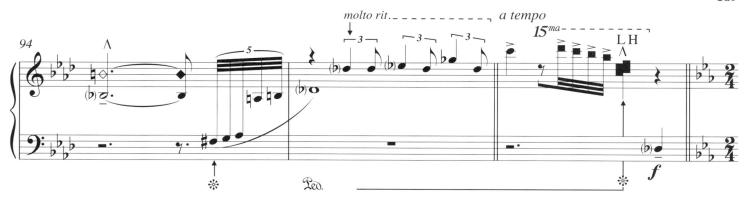

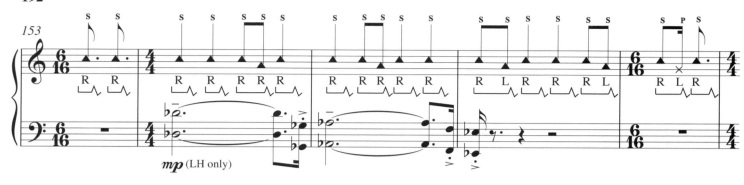

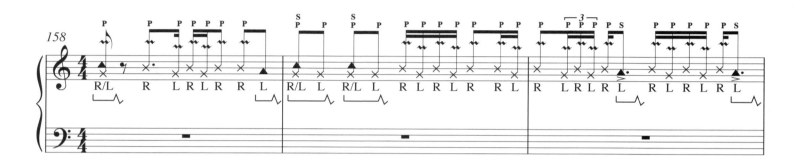

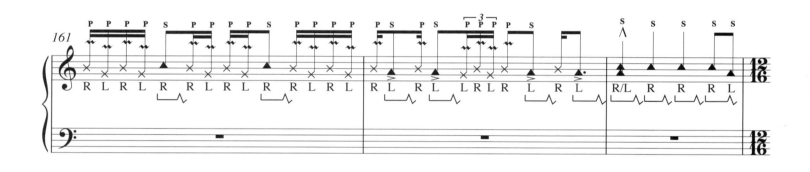

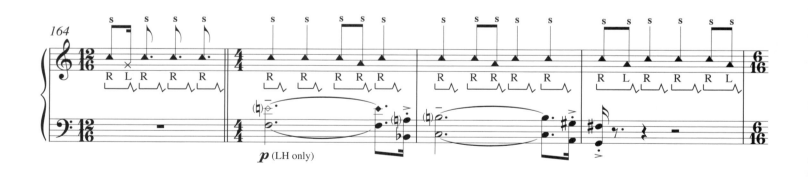

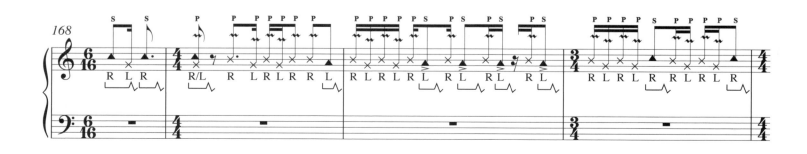

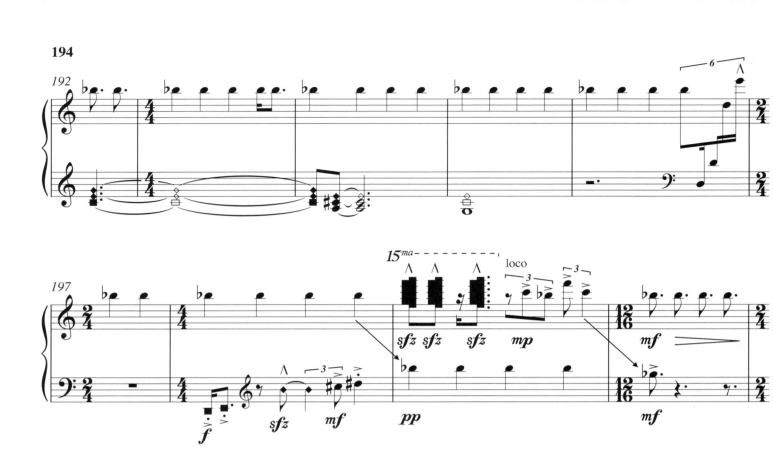

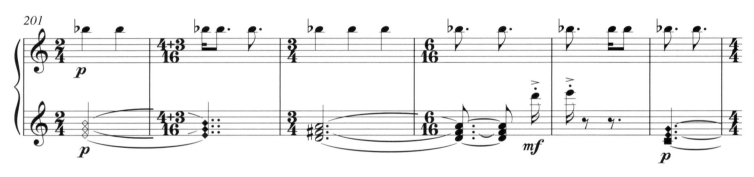

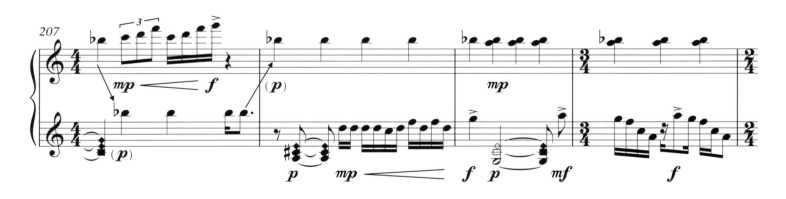

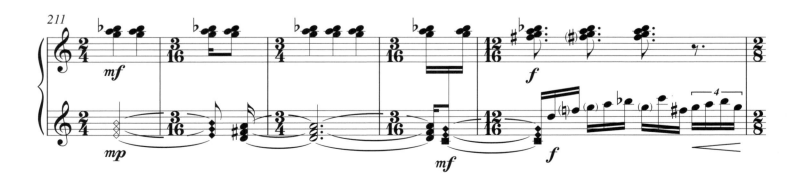

200

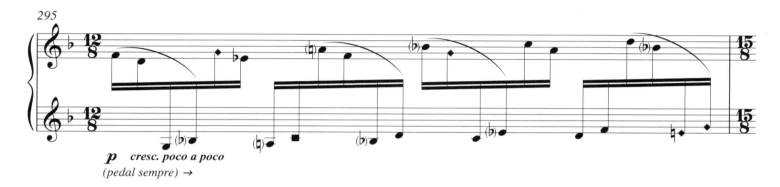

p cresc. poco a poco
(pedal sempre) →

(Sequence: min/Maj 7ths up chromatic starting on G)

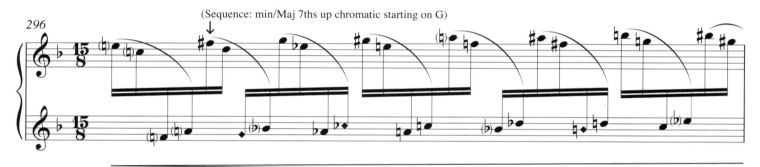

- Princeton, NJ
- Portland, OR
- Sea Ranch, CA
- New York, NY
  (9/20/2013)

In and Out of Love

after "Liaisons" and "Send in the Clowns" from *A Little Night Music*
By Stephen Sondheim and Bernadette Speach

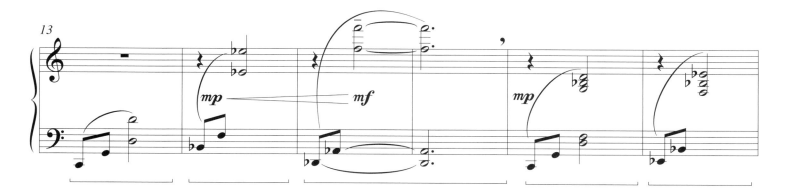

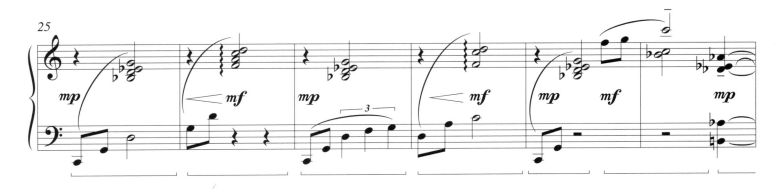

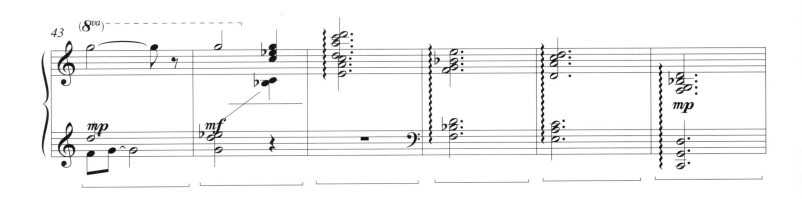

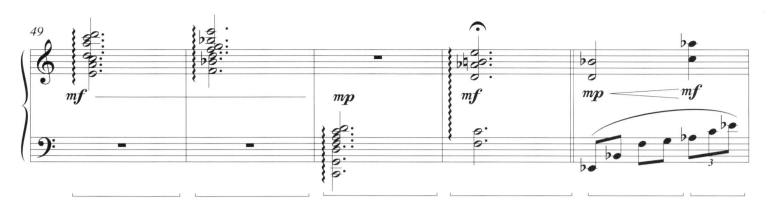

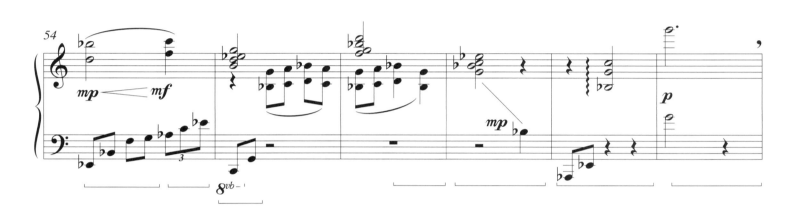

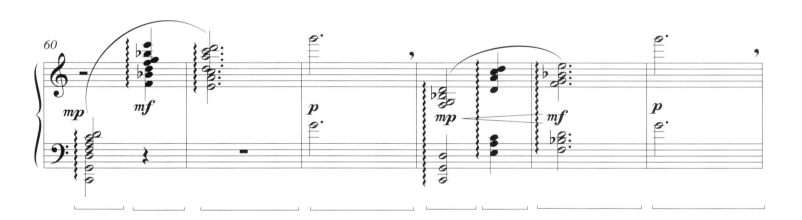

Johanna in Space

after "Johanna" from *Sweeney Todd*
By Stephen Sondheim and Duncan Sheik

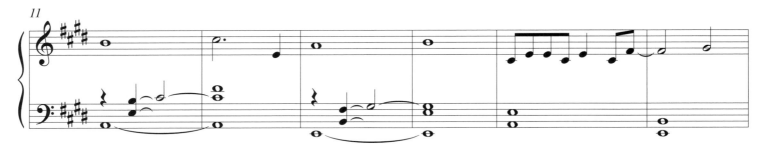

Performance note: Pedal liberally througout. Timings are noted to sync with sound f/x.
See title page for an access code for www.halleonard.com/mylibrary to download or stream companion audio.

The Ladies Who Lunch

after "The Ladies Who Lunch" from *Company*
By Stephen Sondheim and David Rakowski

In Tempo (♩ = 104-112), **a little flexible**

Original tempo

for S.S.

A Little Night Fughetta

after "Anyone Can Whistle" from *Anyone Can Whistle*
and "Send in the Clowns" from *A Little Night Music*
By Stephen Sondheim and William Bolcom

June, 2010
Ann Arbor, MI
Hi Steve!

Love Is in the Air

after "Love Is in the Air" from *A Funny Thing Happened on the Way to the Forum*
By Stephen Sondheim and David Shire

Perkily (♩ = ca. 112)

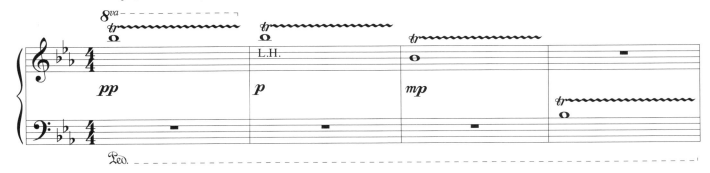

Swing feel (dotted 8th-16ths played as triplets throughout)

with discrete pedal, to taste, throughout

* *Roll tenths wherever necessary throughout.*

(with judicious pedal)

Merrily We Roll Along

after "Merrily We Roll Along" and "The Hills of Tomorrow"
from *Merrily We Roll Along*
By Stephen Sondheim and Nils Vigeland

much pedal

for Ian Gallagher Shearer

No One Is Alone

after "No One Is Alone" from *Into the Woods*
By Stephen Sondheim and Fred Hersch

Not While I'm Around

after "Not While I'm Around" from *Sweeney Todd*
By Stephen Sondheim and Thomas Newman

Notes on "Beautiful"

after "Beautiful" from *Sunday in the Park with George*
By Stephen Sondheim and Rodney Sharman

Dec 1, 2010
Banff

Performance Notes:

Harmonics at the 12th are best played by touching the node on the string with the fingertip close to the dampers. The diamond notehead indicates the pitch that should be heard. The lower note is played on the keyboard.

Use pedal throughout. Follow pedal indications, always allowing some resonance to linger.

The tenuto markings indicate Stephen Sondheim's melody. These notes should be stressed, so that the melodic line is audible.

Now

after "Now," "Later" and "Soon" from *A Little Night Music*
By Stephen Sondheim and Mary Ellen Childs

*playing the G is optional

Paraphrase
(Someone in a Tree)

after "Someone in a Tree" from *Pacific Overtures*
By Stephen Sondheim and Phil Kline

(bring out lower
note in R.H.)

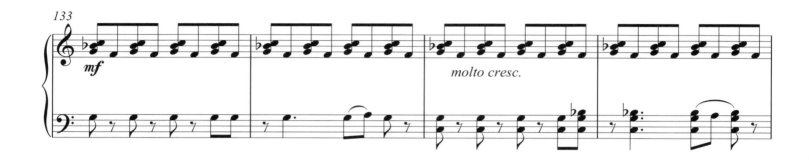

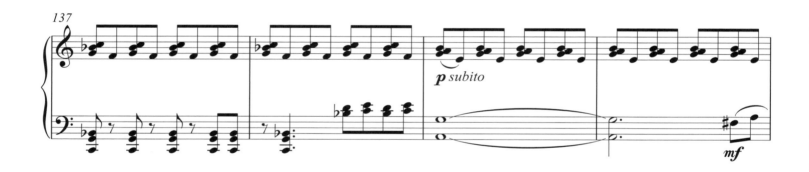

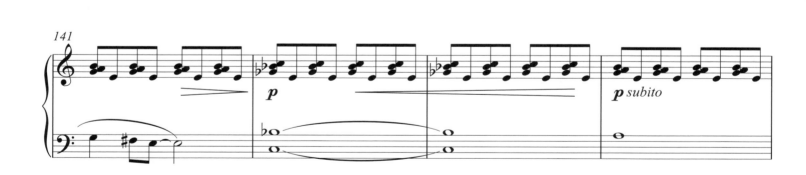

Pretty Women

after "Pretty Women" from *Sweeney Todd*
By Stephen Sondheim and Mark-Anthony Turnage

Pedal lightly

Perpetual Happiness

after "Happiness" from *Passion*
By Stephen Sondheim and Eve Beglarian

NB: Tenuto indicates melody notes in the original song: these want to be brought out lovingly.

Send in the Clowns

after "Send in the Clowns" from *A Little Night Music*
By Stephen Sondheim and Ethan Iverson

Performance Notes

This arrangement will sound best on a shop-worn upright piano.

Ideally, no sustain pedal should be used except for measures 46–51, which swim in pedal. ("What a surprise!
Who could foresee/I'd come to feel about you what you felt about me?")

However, if this arrangement is performed on a concert grand in a difficult hall the pianist may use a bit more pedal.

If it all possible the ritornello should be dry.

The point is to sing the song. Considerable leeway in interpretation is allowed, including changing tempos, rhythms, and even pitches,
 but the tune should always be clear and heartfelt. The left-hand clusters and glissandos can be done different ways.
In measure 59 the glissando may be replaced with a short improvised atonal cadenza.

commissioned by Tom Spain for Anthony de Mare

Sorry/Grateful

after "Sorry-Grateful" from *Company*
By Stephen Sondheim and Derek Bermel

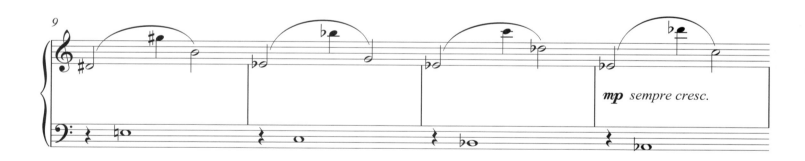

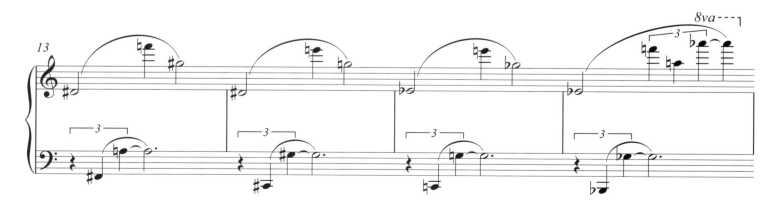

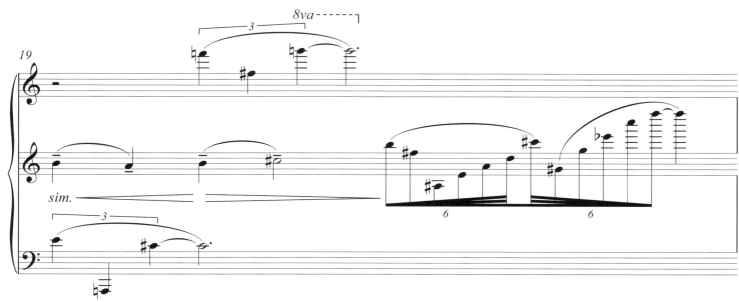

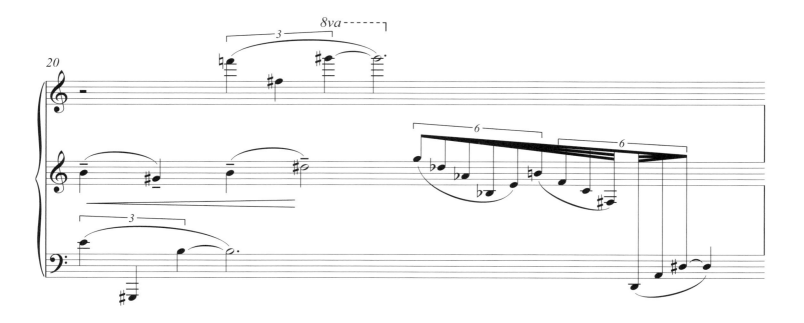

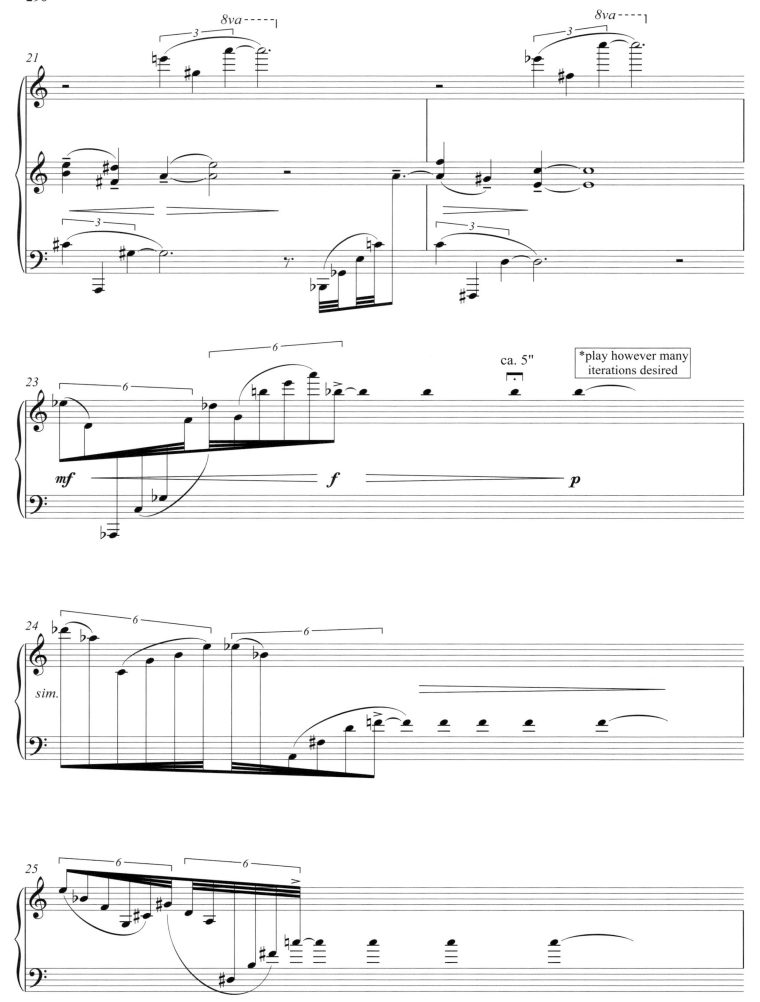

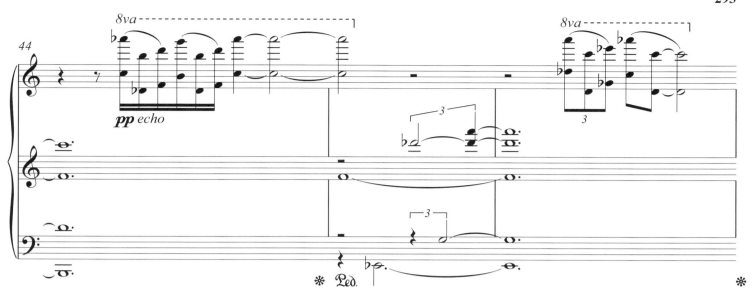

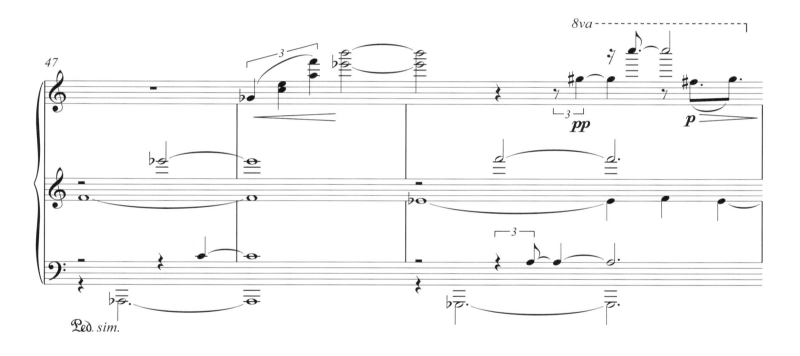

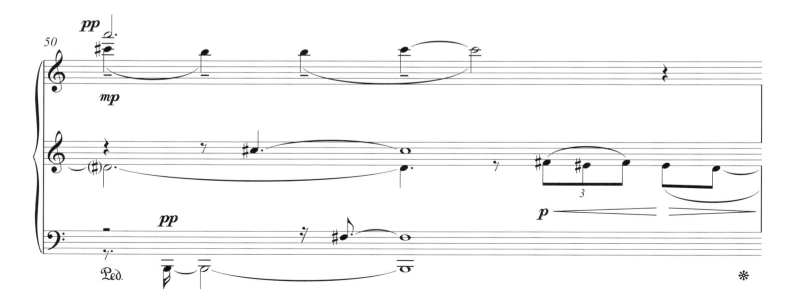

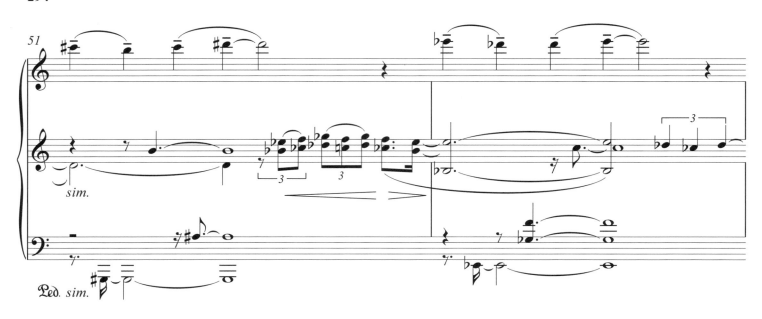

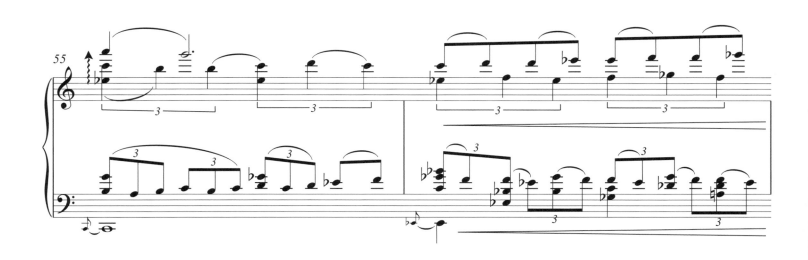

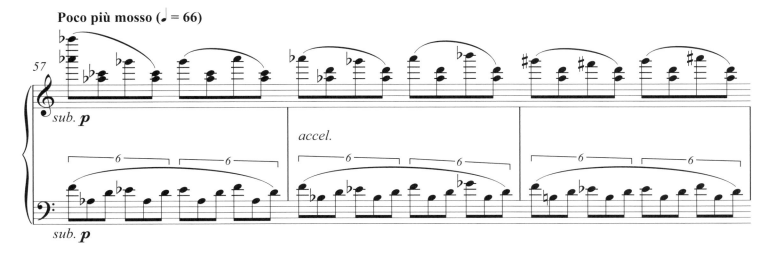

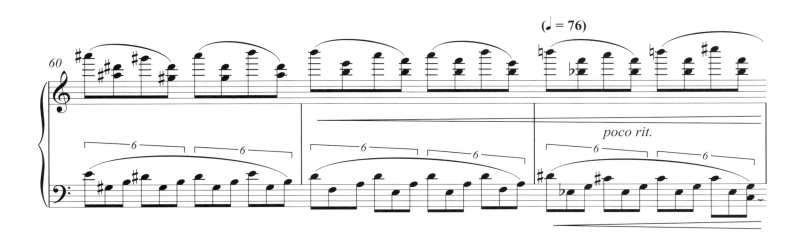

July 2011
Brunswick, ME

That Old Piano Roll

after "That Old Piano Roll" from *Follies*
By Stephen Sondheim and Wynton Marsalis

Sunday in the Park - Passages

after music from *Sunday in the Park with George*
By Stephen Sondheim and Anthony de Mare

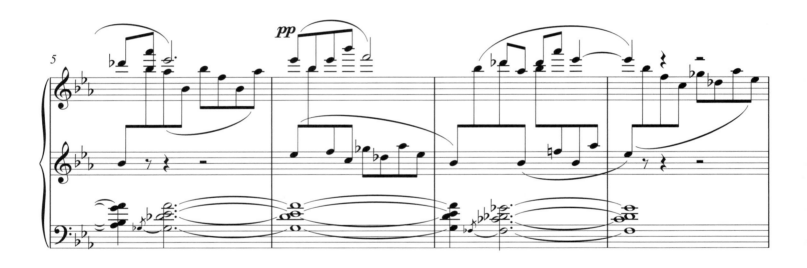

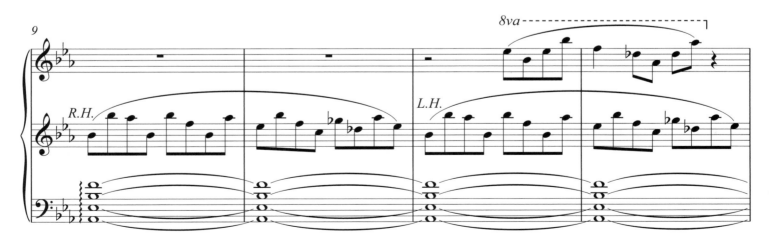

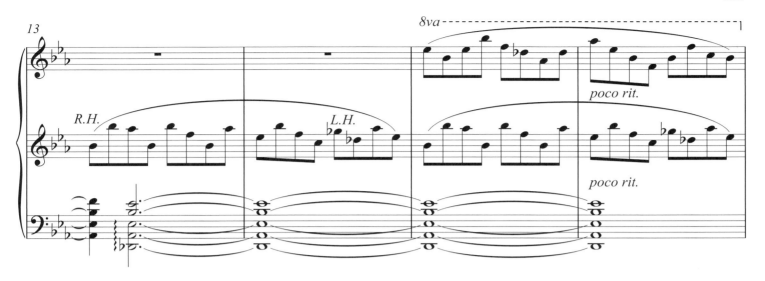

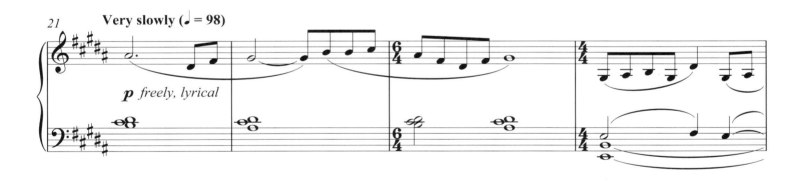

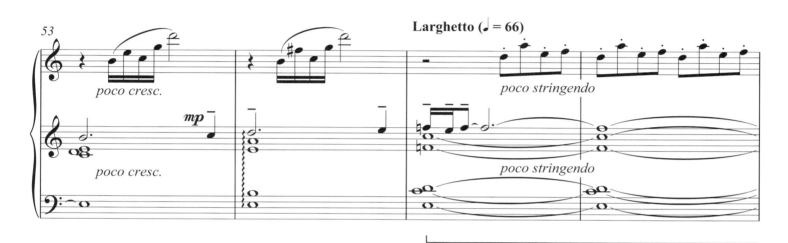

NYC
2009
(rev. 2014)

The Worst [Empanadas] in London

after "The Worst Pies in London" and "A Little Priest" from *Sweeney Todd*
By Stephen Sondheim and Ricardo Lorenz

13

(bring L.H. to the foreground)

ff *sub.* **mp**

L.H. bass lines leads always

(resulting compound rhythm)

continue pedaling freely and discreetly

16

mp

19

21

cresc. – – – – – – –

8ᵛᵇ – – – – – – – – – – – –

Made with meat of pseudo-Latin jazz pianist

bring out the "tune" in R.H.

23

ff *sub.* **mf**

loco

(8ᵛᵇ)

And this one is made
with meat of awful
ballroom tango dancer

Meat of a Tito Puente wannabe

This one made with meat belonging to
merengue dancer with skanky dress

Subito pochissimo più mosso

"Little Priest"
makes its delicious grand entrance

And this last empanda made with
meat from the worst possible joropo dancer

You Could Drive a Person Crazy
(Schizo Scherzo)

after "You Could Drive a Person Crazy" from *Company*
By Stephen Sondheim and Eric Rockwell

(These four measures are easy, so it's a good time to flash a smile at the audience)

Like a Saloon Pianist!
(Very Honky-Tonk)

Commissioned as part of The Liaisons Project by Ellen & Jim Marcus and Annaliese Soros,
in honor of the wedding of Beth Sapery and Rosita Sarnoff.

Very Put Together

after "Putting it Together" from *Sunday in the Park with George*
By Stephen Sondheim and Mason Bates

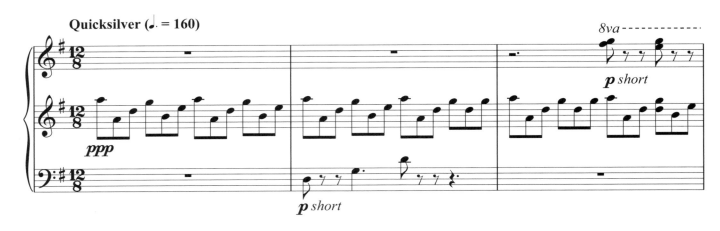

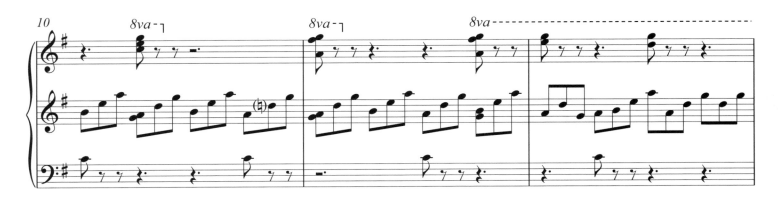

(R.H.)

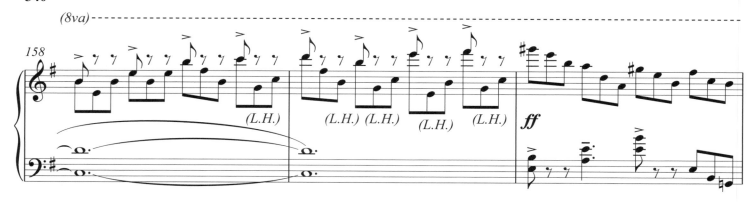